PARTY TIME!

PLAN AN OUTDOOR PARTY

ERIC BRAUN

LERNER PUBLICATIONS COMPANY • MINNEAPOLIS

Lerner Publications Company
A division of Lerner Publishing Group, Inc.
241 First Avenue North
Minneapolis, MN 55401 USA

For reading levels and more information, look up this title at www.lernerbooks.com.

Main text set in Gill Sans MT Std 11/14.
Typeface provided by Monotype Typography.

Library of Congress Cataloging-in-Publication Data

Braun, Eric, 1971- author.
        Plan an outdoor party / by Eric Braun.
            pages   cm. — (Party time!)
        Includes index.
        ISBN 978–1–4677–3833–0 (lib. bdg. : alk. paper)
        ISBN 978–1–4677–4725–7 (eBook)
        1. Children's parties—Planning—Juvenile literature. 2. Entertaining—Planning—Juvenile literature. 3. Outdoor recreation for children—Juvenile literature. I. Title.
        GV1472.7.B5W37 2015
        793.2'1—dc23   2013041261

Manufactured in the United States of America
1 – PC – 7/15/14

TABLE OF CONTENTS

WHY HOST AN OUTDOOR PARTY?

ISN'T SUMMERTIME THE BEST? School is out, and you have lots of free time to relax, play, read, and get a head start on next year's homework (just kidding). Not only that, but the weather is warm, so you can spend plenty of time outdoors without needing to bundle up.

An outdoor party is the perfect way to add a little extra dose of awesome to your summer. At an outdoor party, you can play games such as hide-and-seek and croquet. You can have water balloon fights or a Slip 'n Slide "Most Stylish Wipeout" competition. And of course, you can enjoy delicious food.

Mmmm . . . the food. Whether you're munching on mouthwatering ribs or sinking your teeth into a big, juicy hot dog, food is usually the major focus of any outdoor party. But you don't have to be a carnivore to party in the summer. If meat isn't your thing, you can grill some corn, bell peppers, tomatoes, squash, and other tasty veggies. Or try spicy black bean burgers with all the fixings. You might also opt for a picnic party with a variety of sandwiches with and without meat. The great thing about summertime party food is that there are so many yummy options!

Turn the page to learn all you need to know about outdoor party food, games, decorations, music, and more. Before long, you'll be all set to throw the outdoor party of the summer!

CHAPTER ONE

COOKING UP YOUR COOKOUT

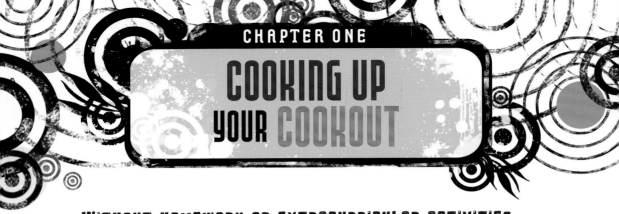

WITHOUT HOMEWORK OR EXTRACURRICULAR ACTIVITIES TO KEEP YOU BUSY, SUMMERTIME CAN FEEL WIIIIIIDE OPEN! The skies are blue, and you've got nothing to do. So you can throw an outdoor party on just about any old day you want, right?

Well, don't be so sure. Lots of kids go to camps or take vacations in the summer. That means you do need to plan ahead. You also might want to plan your party to celebrate a holiday like Memorial Day or Independence Day. Talk it over with your family and find the right date together. It could be that *you* have some vacations or other obligations planned.

Party tip: To help make sure your bash is well attended, check with your friends to see when they have summer activities planned.

GETTING AN ADULT TO SAY YES

For any party, you have to get a parent or another adult in charge to give you permission. In most cases, he or she will have to help you plan, cook, and clean up—even though you should be handling most of the work yourself. After all, it *is* your party!

If you're planning a cookout, the adult will have extra responsibility—mainly, running the grill. Barbecuing requires an adult to cook food over the fire. You also might be preparing complicated recipes that involve marinating food ahead of time and handling raw meat.

marinating = putting meat in a sauce for a period of time before cooking to add flavor

Even if you're not planning to barbecue, an adult's help is important. To help convince your family to let you host a party, let them know that you're responsible enough to deal with all the details. That means taking on the planning, preparing, and—even though it isn't very fun for you—the cleaning! Present a plan that proves you have thought out the party and are capable of doing the work.

Don't forget to keep up with your chores and other responsibilities to show how trustworthy you are. You could even remind your family of your good work: "Dad, I did the dishes every day this week without being asked, and I cleaned out the gecko's aquarium. I've got this!"

TO GRILL OR NOT TO GRILL

That is the question. For many people, nothing is more festive than cooking over a fire and eating grilled goodies with friends. The grilling gives the party a direction—something to look forward to—and grilled food is just plain fun. But if you don't like the idea of licking barbecue sauce off your fingers in front of your guests, you can plan a picnic or even just set out non-grilled food and snacks buffet-style instead.

YOUR GUEST LIST

Talk with the adult in charge about how many kids you can invite. If you're going to have your party in your yard or in, say, a courtyard at your apartment building, think about how much space you have. How quickly will it get crowded? If you are hoping to throw a bigger bash than what you have room for, consider hosting it at a park. You can usually use a shelter or a picnic area at a park for little or no cost. Then you can invite more kids, and you can play games that use more space, like capture the flag or soccer. You might even be able to use horseshoe pits, a volleyball court, a beach, or a swimming pool.

Once you know how many guests you can invite, make your list. This can be tough. You can't invite everyone you know, but you don't want to hurt anyone's feelings either. Remember that the party should be fun, so start your list with kids you have fun with. Then think about mixing kids from different groups. You could invite some friends from scouts and some friends from your softball camp, for example.

One more thought on your guest list: If you have two friends who aren't getting along, think carefully about whom you invite. If you invite both, talk to them ahead of time. Ask them to keep the peace for this event as a favor to you. But if you don't think they can do that, just pick one or the other—or neither. Make a plan to do something with whomever you didn't invite at some other time. You want any friends you aren't inviting to know that you value spending time with them.

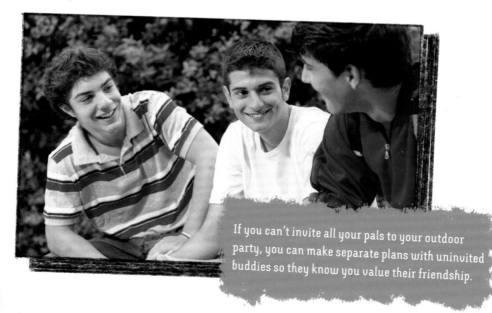

If you can't invite all your pals to your outdoor party, you can make separate plans with uninvited buddies so they know you value their friendship.

YOUR TO-DO LIST

Use a planner or a calendar on a phone to plan your outdoor party and remind you of these dates.

FOUR WEEKS TO GO

- ❑ Ask an adult in charge for permission.
- ❑ Pick out invites.
- ❑ Write a guest list.
- ❑ Choose a party theme.

THREE WEEKS TO GO

- ❑ Send out invites.
- ❑ Plan the menu.
- ❑ Buy or make decorations.

TWO WEEKS TO GO

- ❑ Make sure your friends have RSVP'd (that means they said yes or no).
- ❑ Get the entertainment ready—pick music and plan activities.

ONE WEEK TO GO

- ❑ Hang decorations.
- ❑ Buy food (with an adult's help).
- ❑ Fill the goody bags, if you'll be handing any out.

ONE DAY TO GO

- ❑ Pick out your outfit.
- ❑ Prep the food.
- ❑ Run through the party schedule with an adult in charge.
- ❑ Get ready to party!

INVITES

Do you know when and where your party will be? Good. Do you have your guest list figured out? Excellent. You are now ready to send out invitations.

Lots of people send electronic invites through a website like Evite. Electronic invites are cool because there are many themes to choose from. They're also pretty easy to use as long as everyone on your list has e-mail. If you go with paper invites, you can buy premade ones or make your own. Homemade invites can show a personal touch that can make others more excited about your party.

Your invitation needs to include the following information:

What: What type of party is it? A Memorial Day cookout? A swim party at the park?

When: The date and time of the party

Where: The address of the party

Special information: Let your guests know if there is anything special they need to wear, bring, or come prepared to do. If it's a swim party, they'll need swimsuits and towels. If you're planning a big meal, you might ask people to bring a side dish or a dessert to share.

RSVP: This is an abbreviation of the French phrase for "Please respond." Put your phone number or e-mail address in this section of the invite so your friends can let you know if they're coming.

FLAG INVITATION

If your party is on or near your country's Independence Day (July 1 for Canada, July 4 for the United States), it can be fun to make invitations that look like your country's flag. For a US flag, cut sheets of printer paper into quarters and use each quarter as an invitation. Cut out red stripes from construction paper and glue them across the rectangle. Then add a square of blue construction paper in the corner. You can draw stars with a white crayon or apply star stickers. You won't be able to fit all fifty stars, but it will look good. On the back, write the information for your party.

YOU'RE INVITED TO SHAWN'S INDEPENDENCE DAY BASH!

WHEN: SATURDAY, JULY 4TH, 3:30–11 P.M.
WHERE: 1234 BLACKBERRY RD, ANYTOWN USA 55555

Come at 3:30 for a water balloon fight and rides on my uncle's boat. Wear your swimsuit and bring a change of clothes. Swim shoes are required in the lake. We'll have a cookout at 6:30 and watch the fireworks from the pier at sunset.

RSVP: SHAWN JONES 555-321-5555

Here's a sample of a party invitation for an outdoor party.

ACTIVITIES AND OTHER FUN STUFF TO DO

You have lots of options for fun things to do at an outdoor party. You're not confined to a small space inside, and you don't have to worry as much about noise and mess. Guests can feel free to run around and have a blast! Here's a list of just a few things you can do at an outdoor party:

➡ **PLAY LAWN GAMES** such as beanbag toss (also known as cornhole), croquet, badminton, and boccie ball.

➡ **PLAY IN THE WATER**—for instance, run through a sprinkler, play Marco Polo in a pool, or hold a water balloon toss contest.

➡ **PLAY PARK GAMES** such as tag, hide-and-seek, kickball, horseshoes, capture the flag, and ships across the ocean.

➡ Even though you're outside, sometimes a quieter activity is a nice way to balance things out. *Consider charades, trivia, Mad Libs, or a craft.*

Party tip: If you have more people than equipment, form teams and have people rotate turns. Don't let anyone feel left out.

COME UP WITH A SCHEDULE

You'll want to plan your party so you don't try to pack in too much activity. Your plan might look something like this:

★ 3:00 p.m.—Guests arrive. Eat snacks and hang out.

★ 3:30 p.m.—Huge game of capture the flag!

★ 4:30 p.m.—Do a craft.

★ 5:30 p.m.—Eat dinner.

★ 6:00 p.m.—Play charades.

★ 7:00 p.m.—Party ends. Be sure to send your guests home with any tasty leftover snacks!

Making a party schedule helps ensure you leave enough time for each fun activity—like water fights!

FOOD AND TREATS

As you know, food is a big deal at an outdoor party. You'll want to plan ahead carefully with an adult so that your food-serving plans go off without a hitch. Make as much of the food ahead of time as you can. Here are some make-ahead snacks that aren't too daunting:

- ☆ Cut-up veggies and fruit (put the fruit in a carved-out watermelon for an extra fun touch!)
- ☆ Sandwiches or wraps
- ☆ Tortilla chips and salsa or potato chips with onion dip
- ☆ Ants on a log—that is, celery sticks with peanut butter and raisins
- ☆ Pita chips and hummus

If you're going to grill, make sure the food you'll be grilling is set to go and that the adult is ready to do the cooking. Also, remember that for foods like hamburgers and hot dogs, you'll need to set out condiments, sliced buns, and other ingredients such as sliced tomatoes and pickles.

condiments = something used to make food more flavorful, such as ketchup, mustard, and relish

If hamburgers and hot dogs are on your menu, make sure you also provide vegetarian options for guests who might want them. This doesn't have to be complicated. You can even just pick up some veggie patties in the grocery store. Most stores have these in their freezer sections.

Party tip: Fresh veggies such as corn, zucchini, and peppers also taste great cooked on the grill. Go online or to a library to find recipes.

As for drinks, it's fun and easy to put cans of soda or bottles of water in a cooler of ice where kids can help themselves. Carbonated water with natural fruit flavoring is a nice option for those who don't want the sugar or the caffeine that comes in many sodas.

Party tip: Don't have a cooler? Cover a laundry basket with a clean plastic garbage bag and fill with ice—instant drink cooler!

You can handle dessert and treats in a similarly simple way. Get a few boxes of Popsicles or ice-cream sandwiches that you can pass out after the meal. Other fun ideas include an ice-cream cake, cookies, cupcakes, or—for a healthful treat—frozen smoothies made with real fruit.

Finally, find out if any of your friends have allergies or other food sensitivities, and be sure to provide food for them too. For example, you could serve rice crackers for friends who can't eat gluten. Or you could serve fresh tomato salsa instead of cheese dip with your chips if one of your guests is allergic to dairy.

gluten = a protein found in wheat

DECORATIONS

Decorations make a party feel like a party—and decorating is fun to do! What's your decorating personality? Do you like to go wild with the decorations, or are you more of a keep-it-simple kind of kid? Either way is fine. Keep in mind how much time and money you want to spend and make a plan.

If your party is at home, you can parcel out the work ahead of time so it's not a last-minute worry. If you're partying at a park or somewhere else, plan to arrive early to decorate. Here are some ideas for decorating for an outdoor party. You can probably think of more.

⇨ String the trees with outdoor lights or set out solar-powered lanterns if your party will go into the evening.

⇨ Hang bunting, streamers, or banners on walls or from beams.

⇨ Weigh down bunches of colorful helium-filled balloons with small sandbags (you can get these at a party store) or stones.

PEST PROBLEMS

If mosquitoes are common where you live, you will want to plan a way to keep them away. Burn citronella candles, which, when it gets dark, will look cool while keeping the biting pests at bay. You might also want to provide mosquito repellent that guests can spray on themselves if needed. Choose a nonirritating repellent with little or no scent.

➡ Cover the table with a colorful tablecloth or poster paper. Toss some confetti across the table too!

➡ Display fresh-cut flowers or even cuttings from your yard, like pussy willow branches.

➡ Buy festive paper plates, cups, and napkins. These are not only nice decorations, but they help cleanup go a lot faster because you don't have to wash as many dishes.

Party tip: If your party is in a park or outdoor spot away from home, figure out how you will get decorations to the location (and how you'll put them up) *before* the day of the party.

You probably want to have music at your party too. Work with an adult or a friend to figure out how to play music outside if you don't have a system for doing so. A portable MP3 player dock is an easy solution for home or the park. If it's not battery-powered, make sure you'll have an outlet handy. You may need to get an extension cord. Make up a long party mix of music that you and your friends will enjoy. That way, you won't have to keep changing the music during the party—when you should be paying attention to your guests.

CHAPTER TWO

IT'S TIME TO PARTY!

THE BIG DAY IS HERE, BUT YOU CAN'T SIT BACK AND PARTY JUST YET. There are a few more things to take care of before your guests arrive.

✓ Mow the lawn if you have one—or ask the adult in charge to do it if he or she would rather not have you use the lawn mower.

✓ Pick up any toys, tools, or anything else in the yard. This includes dog poop. After all, no one wants to step into a stinky mess!

✓ Clean the kitchen and any bathrooms your guests will use. Even though it's an outdoor party, people will need to come in at least occasionally.

✓ Prepare all the food and set it out.

✓ Make sure the decorating is done.

A freshly mowed lawn is a welcoming sight at any outdoor party.

✓ Set up your games, activities, and tunes.

✓ Make sure you have a trash can and recycling bin in an easy-to-access place.

Next, check out the seating situation. If you're partying at home, make sure you have a place for everyone to sit. If you don't have a chair for everyone, throw a couple of nice blankets in the grass where people can hang out.

GREET YOUR GUESTS

If the party is in your backyard, put a sign on your front door that tells guests to go around back. Or assign a family member or a friend to greet them there and send them back.

Hosting a party means making sure everyone feels welcome and is having fun. Say hi to each of your guests as they arrive. Smile and tell them individually how glad you are that they could come. If they brought anything like food or swim stuff, show them where they can put it.

Show your guests the food and tell them about the activities you'll be doing at the party. As people begin to mix, introduce those who don't know one another. If you've invited kids from different groups, like from your summer camp and your school, explain how you know each of them and help them find things they have in common to talk about.

Party tip: Contests and games are great ways to break the ice and get the party started. Offer some fun prizes as incentives to get everyone to join in!

have siblings, figure out ahead of time how much you want them to be
of your party. If you want a no-siblings party, ask your family to help
e for them to have a playdate at someone's house. If your friends know
e your siblings, it might be fine to let them hang out. In that case, give
a job like serving drinks or keeping the snack bowls full. That will keep
occupied and happy.

have a dog that jumps on people, plan to keep that from happening. Put
room with something to chew on, but don't forget to let it out to go to
throom once or twice. Or see if you can get someone to take the dog
g the party.

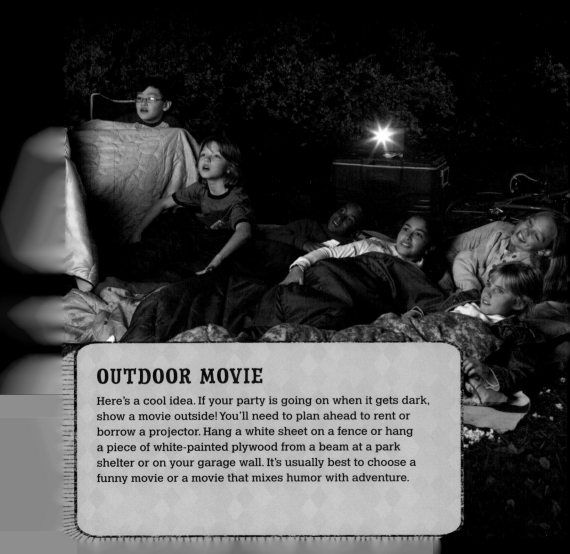

OUTDOOR MOVIE

Here's a cool idea. If your party is going on when it gets dark,
show a movie outside! You'll need to plan ahead to rent or
borrow a projector. Hang a white sheet on a fence or hang
a piece of white-painted plywood from a beam at a park
shelter or on your garage wall. It's usually best to choose a
funny movie or a movie that mixes humor with adventure.

LET'S SET A FEW GROUND RULES

You might think rules are a drag. And if you're having a party, rules are probably the last thing you want to worry about. But rules are important. Sometimes, kids + party = wild behavior. Your family will appreciate it if you keep things under control. To make sure the adult in charge will let you have another party someday, let everyone know the following:

» **Where they can go, and where they can't (stay out of Mom's flower garden!)**

» **Where they can go indoors**

» **Who's allowed to work things like the grill and the stereo**

» **If you're at a pool, any rules about pool behavior**

» **How loudly you can play the music**

Talk about the ground rules beforehand with whoever is in charge, and make sure you and that person both agree on them. When it comes to sharing the rules with your guests, be firm, but always be polite. After all, nobody has fun when being ordered around.

Party tip: Live bands or djs can make a party rock, but be considerate to your neighbors. Let them know about your party and how long it will last. Also, some areas have laws about outside noise. Have an adult help you check out what rules you need to follow so there won't be any problems during your party.

HAVE FUN—WITH EVERYONE

Now that your party is kickin', it's time to have some fun. Spend time with all your guests, chatting, snacking, and playing. But don't forget to make sure everyone else is having fun too. If someone doesn't seem to be enjoying herself, talk to her. Ask if she wants to join you in a game. Try to connect different groups that have something in common to talk about.

Party tip: Outdoor sports can be fun, but not everyone loves athletic activities. Give those who'd rather not play the job of scorekeeper so that they are included in the game. Or "hire" them as photographers and give an awesome prize for the best action shot!

WE LOVE OUTDOOR PARTIES BECAUSE WE LOVE THE OUTDOORS

It's true! So why not support the outdoors by adding a "green" element to your party? For example, have everyone pick up at least one piece of trash at the park where you're holding your party. Or ask your guests to bring a small donation if they want to, and you can give the cash to an environmental group like the World Wildlife Fund. At the end of the party, give everyone a fun Earth-friendly gift like a packet of seeds they can plant, a reusable shopping bag, or a steel water bottle.

Do your best to stay on your schedule. (See page 13.) But use it as a guide, not the law. If people are starving, don't be afraid to start the meal early. If people are having a blast dancing, don't cut off the music just because the schedule says it's time for s'mores. Your party will take on a life of its own.

Don't forget to sit back and enjoy your bash!

HERE'S A *super-duper important* **RULE ABOUT YOUR PARTY:** make sure you have fun! That's the whole reason you did this, right? So sure, you need to make sure people are getting along and following the rules. You need to make sure the food is ready on time and the dog isn't biting your friends. But in between all that, try to relax! Smile and be charming! These people came to your party because they like you, so go ahead and be the life of the party. After all, if *you're* having fun, everyone else probably will too.

CHAPTER THREE

AFTER THE PARTY

BEFORE YOU KNOW IT, YOUR PARTY WILL BE DRAWING TO A CLOSE. If everyone had a great time, they might be reluctant to leave. That just goes to show what an awesome party planner you are! Still, even the best parties have to end sometime, so start letting people know when the end is coming up. That way, they won't be surprised when it's time to go. You can say something like, "This has been such a blast! I can't wait to do it again soon."

Party tip: A toast is a great way to let everyone know you are glad they came to the party.

GIVEAWAYS

You might decide to have goody bags or a take-home item for every guest. Take-homes are not necessary, but if you decide to do them for your outdoor party, here are some ideas:

* ★ *Glamorous sunglasses*
* ★ Costume jewelry
* ★ Hair accessories for girls—barrettes, elastic headbands, or beads
* ★ **CARDS:** sports trading cards, Pokémon cards, Magic cards, or regular playing cards
* ★ **A group photo** of everyone at the party (you might need to send this later)
* ★ CANDY
* ★ A MIX CD YOU MADE
* ★ A book or a notebook

If you use a bag to hold your goodies, add crinkled paper shreds on top to add some mystery and color.

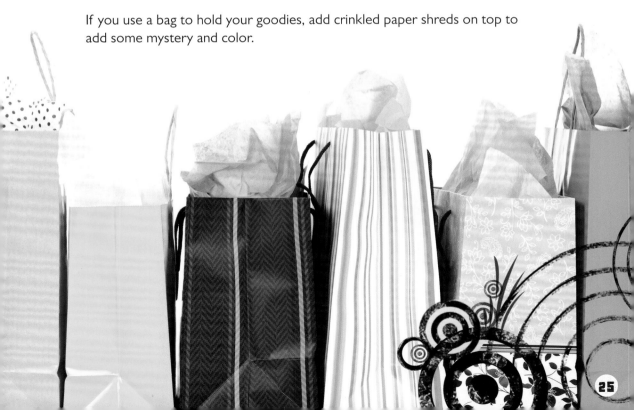

CLEANUP TIME

Well, you knew this part of the night was coming eventually. Don't feel overwhelmed! Just turn on some music and get started. Music keeps your attitude positive and makes the job less boring. If it's late, of course, make sure to play the music softly. Sleeping family members and neighbors don't want to be jolted out of bed by 1D (as much as you may love them)!

Take a look at what you have to do, and break the work down into parts. You're going to have dishes to clean and food to put away. You'll have trash and recycling to clean up and tables to wipe down. You'll need to take down those decorations and either toss them or store them for next time. If there is food on the ground, make sure to pick it up. That will keep pests away and prevent any dogs (either yours or someone else's) from eating something they shouldn't.

Party tip: You can make cleanup time fun—or at least make it seem like less of a chore. Ask your bestie if she or he can stick around to help, or offer a prize to a sibling to help you after the party.

Thanking your friends for coming lets them know you enjoyed their presence.

THANK-YOU NOTES

Are you glad everyone came to your party? Hey, if nobody came, it wouldn't have been a party! One extra-nice way to show your appreciation is to send thank-you notes. This certainly isn't a must, but it's definitely a nice touch.

Just like with invitations, you can buy thank-you cards from the store or you can make your own. Or you can send a friendly e-mail or even a simple text. If anyone helped out by bringing food or gifts, make sure to send that person a handwritten thank-you. In that case, a written thank-you *is* required. When a guest goes all out, so should you!

THAT WAS A BLAST!

Being a good party host can be stressful, but if you plan ahead, the stress melts away and what's left is fun. That means it's totally worth it! If your friends have a good time at your party, you'll all be telling stories about it for a long time. Congratulations—you're a memory-making friend. Your middle name should be "party."

OUTDOOR PARTY THEME IDEAS

A party's a party, right? Well, sometimes a party is more than a party—if it has the right theme. For example, how about hosting an island luau party, where everyone wears grass skirts, drinks out of coconut-shaped cups, and does the limbo by the light from paper lanterns? Or a rain forest theme with decorations that look like trees, monkeys, and waterfalls; leaf-shaped cookies; and opportunities to donate to a rain forest preservation organization? Here are a few other ideas:

SAFARI THEME

Provide safari helmets (those hats with a round top and a wide brim), and organize a "safari" where teams of kids follow clues to find a prize. Decorate for the party with jungle-themed images.

SNOW CONE THEME

Rent a shaved icemaker, and buy a bunch of different flavors of syrup. Then let kids make their own snow cones.

INDEPENDENCE DAY THEME

Ask everyone to dress in patriotic colors and play patriotic music. Play a trivia game about your country's history.

CAMPING THEME

Have an adult build a bonfire, and let everyone roast marshmallows and make s'mores. Have everyone cuddle under blankets by the fire and tell ghost stories—or funny stories! Put out camping lanterns, and pitch a tent in the yard to use as a game room.

BEACH THEME

Play beach volleyball while listening to beach music. Decorate with ocean images and beach balls. Have your guests make construction-paper fish or paper-plate crabs (here are some instructions for the latter: http://www.ehow.com /how_4501593_make-paper-plate-crab.html). Send everyone home with a beach bucket full of beach toys.

THE PERFECT OUTDOOR PARTY PLAYLIST

No outdoor party is complete without the perfect playlist to keep everyone in a party mood. You can't go wrong if you add these tunes to your mix:

"Where Have You Been?," Rihanna

"More Than This," One Direction

"Boyfriend," Justin Bieber

"Night and Day," Hot Chip

"Good Time," Owl City featuring Carly Rae Jepsen

"Summertime Clothes," Animal Collective

"The Only Place," Best Coast

FURTHER INFORMATION

KidsHealth: Recipes and Cooking
http://kidshealth.org/kid/recipes/index.html
One of the most reliable sources for health information for kids provides a wide range of healthful recipes kids can make themselves.

Lundsten, Apryl. *A Smart Girl's Guide to Parties.* Middleton, WI: American Girl, 2010.
This book for girls contains all kinds of advice and tips for hosting and attending parties.

O'Bryan, Sharon. *Old Fashioned Children's Games: Over 200 Outdoor, Car Trip, Song, Card, and Party Activities.* Jefferson, NC: McFarland, 2013.
Learn classic games like Kick the Can, Circle Tag, Blind Man's Bluff, and more that will add fun to your party.

Watson, Stephanie. *Plan a Birthday Party.* Minneapolis: Lerner Publications, 2015.
Even if it's not your birthday for a while yet, it's never too early to start planning for your special day!

INDEX

PHOTO ACKNOWLEDGMENTS

The images in this book are used with the permission of: backgrounds © iStockphoto.com/Nenochka (geometric pattern) and © iStockphoto.com/IntergalacticDesignStudio (rolled ink frame); © Bormotov/Dreamstime.com, p. 1; © Bikeriderlondon/Shutterstock.com, p. 4; © iStockphoto.com/Barsik, p. 5; © Big Cheese Photo LLC/Alamy, p. 6; © Michael Blann/Photodisc/Thinkstock, p. 8; © Newcomer/Shutterstock.com, p. 11 (inset); © J. Helgason/Shutterstock.com, p. 11 (background); © DreamPictures/Blend Images/Getty Images, p. 12; © Mike Kemp/Blend Images/Brand X Pictures/Getty Images, p. 13; © Lew Robertson/Photographer's Choice/Getty Images, p. 14; © iStockphoto.com/Sampsyseeds, p. 15; © E.G. Pors/Shutterstock.com, p. 15 (inset); © Eurobanks/Shutterstock.com, p. 16 (background); © Siri Stafford/Iconica/Getty Images, p. 17; © Emde/Dreamstime.com, p. 18; © Hill Street Studios/Brand X Pictures/Getty Images, p. 19; © Christopher Robbins/Iconica/Getty Images, p. 20; © Adrian Weinbrecht/The Image Bank/Getty Images, p. 21; © Monkey Business Images/Collection/Thinkstock, p. 22 (top); © Alistar Berg/Iconica/Getty Images, p. 22 (bottom); © DreamPictures/The Image Bank/Getty Images, p. 23; © Jupiterimages/Stockbyte/Thinkstock, p. 24; © Elena Elisseeva/Shutterstock.com, p. 25; © Hero Images/Getty Images, p. 26; © Ron Levine/Digital Vision/Getty Images, p. 27; © iStockphoto.com/whitewish, p. 28; © A_Lein/Shutterstock.com, p. 29 (top); © Jopelka/Shutterstock.com, p. 29 (bottom).

Front cover: © Jacqueline Veissid/BlendImages/Getty Images.